My Picture Dictionary

by Hale C. Reid
Helen W. Crane

XEROX

Ginn and Company
A Xerox Education Company

Aa Bb Cc Dd

Ee Ff Gg Hh

Ii Jj Kk Ll

Mm Nn Oo Pp

Qq Rr Ss Tt

Uu Vv Ww Xx

Yy Zz

Home Office, Lexington, Massachusetts 02173
0–663–22171–4

A a

airport

apple

am

an

and

another

any

are

around

as

asked

at

ate

away

a

about

across

after

again

all

always

Bb

baby

baseball

bag

basket

ball

bear

balloon

bed

barn

bee

B b

bell

bicycle

bird

birthday

boat

book

box

boys

bread

brook

B b

bug

bunny

bus

button

back
be

because
best
better
big
bite
bring
build
bump
but
buy
buzzed
by

C c

cake

chair

candle

chicks

candy

children

car

circus

cat

clock

C c

clown

coat

cookies

corn

cowboy

call

came

can

can't

catch

city

cold

color

come

coming

could

crying

D d

dog

doll

dress

duck

eggs

| day |
| did |
| didn't |
| dinner |
| do |
| don't |
| down |
| drop |

E e

| eat |
| every |

F f

farm

flowers

father

feather

fire

fish

fast
faster
find
for
found
friend
frisky
from
fun
funny

G g

girls

goat

grandfather

grandmother

groceries

game

gave

get

getting

give

go

going

gone

good

good-by

got

guess

Hh

hamburger

hand

hat

heart

helicopter

hen

hill

home

honey

horn
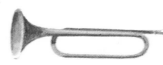

H h

horse

house

had
happen
happy
has
have
he

hear
heard
hello
help
her
here
hide
him
his
hot
how
hurry

ice

ice cream

iron

I
if
I'm
in
into
is
it

J j

jeep

jet

jingle
job
jump
just

K k

key

kitten

king

knife

kitchen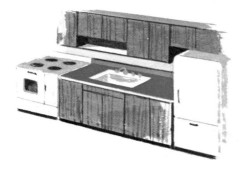

keep

kept

kind

knew

knock

know

kite

15

L l

lamb

leaves

letter

lion

lunch

laughed

learn

let

let's

like

little

live

long

look

lost

lot

love

Mm

mailbox

money

man

moon

meat

mother

milk

mountain

mitten

Mm

mouse

machine
made
make
many
may
maybe
me
men
met

middle
might
mill
miss
more
morning
most
Mr.
Mrs.
much
must
my

nail

nest

newspaper

nickel

nuts

name

need

never

new

next

nice

night

no

noise

not

nothing

now

Oo

ocean

orange

owl

o'clock

of

off

often

oh

old

on

once

only

open

or

other

our

out

over

own

Pp

pan

pancakes

paper

park

pencil

pennies

people

pets

picnic

pig

P p

pocket

pole

policeman

pony

postman

puppy

paint

party

plant

play

please

pop

pretty

puddle

put

Q q

quarter

queen

quack
question
quick
quiet

R r

rabbit

rain

rooster

race
ran
ready
ride
ring
rolled
run

S s

saddle

seesaw

Santa Claus

sheep

satellite

shoe

school

skate

scissors

sky

S s

sled

snake

snow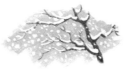

snowman

sprinkler

squirrel

star

store

street

streetcar

S s

sun

said

sang

sat

saw

say

see

shall

she

side

sing

sleep

so

some

something

soon

splash

started

stay

step

stop

story

surprise

Tt

table

taxi

teacher

teeth

telephone

television

top

town

toys

tractor

T t

train

tree

truck

turkey

turtle

take
than
thank
that
the
their
them
then
there
they
thing
think

T t

this	today
three	tomorrow
time	too
tiny	took
to	two

U u

umbrella

up
us

V v

valentine

very

visiting

W w

wagon

window

watch

wolf

wheat

woman

wheel

woods

whistle

world

W w

wait	what
walk	when
want	where
warm	who
was	will
wash	win
water	wish
way	with
we	wonderful
well	word
went	work
were	would

X x

xylophone

x as in:

box

fox

Y y

yard

yes

you

your

Z z

zoo

zero

zoom

Action Words

climb

hop

run

swim

swing

skip

dance

walk

jump

skate

Parts of the Body

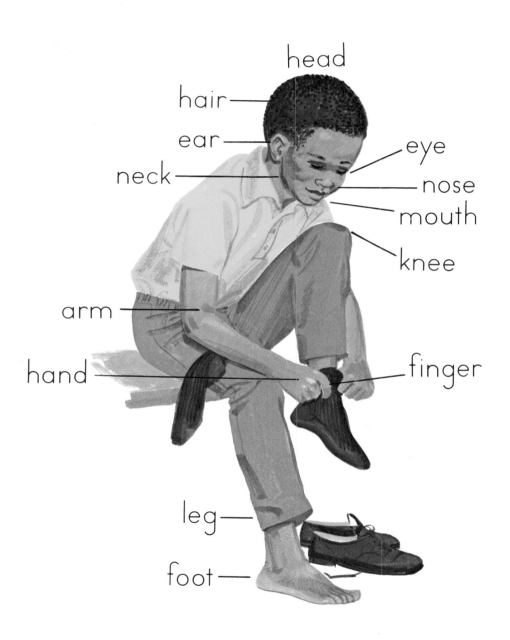

head

hair—

ear—

neck—

eye

nose

mouth

knee

arm —

hand —

finger

leg—

foot—

The Family

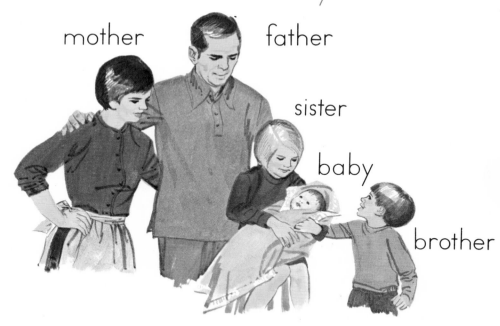

mother father sister baby brother

cousins aunt uncle

grandmother grandfather

Toys

doll   kite   drum

train   ball

car   truck   boat

wagon   bicycle

Helpful Little Words

across

between

into

on

up

in   out

down

over

under

Farm

haystack

tractor

silo

barn

farmhouse

pump

pigs

fence

garden

cow

grass

calf

chickens

pony

City

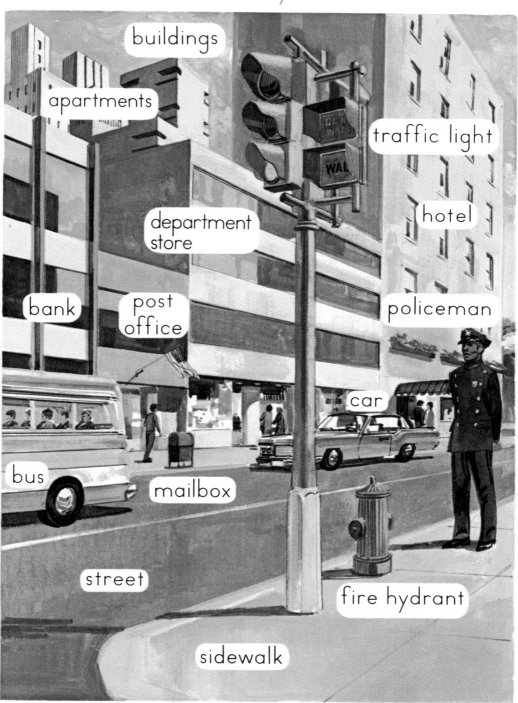

buildings

apartments

traffic light

department store

hotel

bank

post office

policeman

car

bus

mailbox

street

fire hydrant

sidewalk

Fruits

plum   orange   lemon

banana   grapes

cherry   pear   apple

strawberry   peach

Vegetables

potato   peas   onion

celery   squash

beans   beet   cabbage

lettuce   carrot

Weather

moon   stars   sun

snow   sky

wind   clouds   rain

lightning   rainbow

Kinds of Workers

farmer

nurse

fireman

policeman

pilot

bus driver

dentist

clerk

teacher

milkman

doctor

mailman

Animals

rabbit

bear

monkey

fox

raccoon

elephant

seal

tiger

lion

beaver

Number Zoo

1 one

2 two

3 three

4 four

5 five

6 six

7 seven

8 eight

9 nine

10 ten

Days of the Week

Sunday
Monday
Tuesday
Wednesday
Thursday
Friday
Saturday

Colors

yellow   green   blue   orange

red   brown   white   black

Months and Holidays

January
New Year's Day

February
Valentine's Day

March

April

May
Mother's Day

June
Father's Day

July

Fourth of July

August

September

October
Halloween

November
Thanksgiving Day

December
Christmas Day

47

NOTE TO PARENTS AND TEACHERS

My Picture Dictionary is designed to help the small child help himself in writing and spelling. It also introduces the dictionary habit, which can and should be encouraged as early as the First Grade. As children use the illustrations to locate words in this simple dictionary, they learn that words (1) have printed symbols and (2) can be arranged alphabetically. Usually this experience is their first contact with words in an alphabetical arrangement.

Selection of Content

The 175 nouns illustrated in this dictionary were selected from 2800 different words found in 4500 independently written compositions of 1500 first-grade children. The additional 272 words in the body of the dictionary are among those which appeared with the highest frequencies in these compositions. The entire word list has been closely correlated with the vocabulary of the early books in the Reading 360 Program, as well as the GINN BASIC READING SERIES.

Included in this dictionary are also sixteen classification pages of pictured words such as "Toys," "Fruits," and "Animals." These pages add 132 more words to the dictionary.

Format

The pictured words are listed first under each guide letter. The words that do not lend themselves to illustration are alphabetized separately in easily distinguishable columns.

The entries are in manuscript writing such as the child will be learning and using. The single-word entry makes it easy for the first- or second-grade child to find the words he needs in his early composition work. Guide letters, both capital and small, help the child locate the word he wants to write.

The illustrations appear below or beside the entry words. Their simplicity helps a pupil acquire precise meanings.

Suggestions for Helping Children

When a child asks for the spelling of a word, help him to identify the initial letter, as *b* in *boat*. Then help him to find the pages on which the words beginning with that letter are pictured.

Using the dictionary to find out how words are spelled will help him recognize that words beginning with the same sound often start with the same letter.

Although it is not necessary for a child to know the alphabet to look up a word, he will soon learn it through constant use.

The use of *My Picture Dictionary* enables pupils to progress at their own speed in writing activities and thus helps the teacher to provide for individual needs and abilities.

PRINTED IN THE UNITED STATES OF AMERICA

E F G H I J K   7 6 5 4